bright spark

brilliant brain

cool kid

superstar

great work

amazing work

I Can Learn
Handwriting Skills

Written by Brenda Apsley
Illustrated by John Haslam

This book belongs to
....

EGMONT

Tips for happy home learning

Make learning fun by working at your child's pace and always giving tasks which s/he can do. Tasks that are too difficult will discourage her/him from trying again.

⭐

Give encouragement and praise and remember to award gold stars and sticker badges for effort as well as good work.

⭐

Always do too little rather than too much, and finish each session on a positive note.

⭐

Don't work when you or your child is tired or hungry.

⭐

Reinforce workbook activities and new ideas by making use of real objects around the home.

EGMONT
We bring stories to life

Copyright © 2007 Egmont UK Limited
All rights reserved.
Published in Great Britain by Egmont UK Limited,
239 Kensington High Street, London W8 6SA
www.egmont.co.uk

Printed in Italy.
ISBN 978 1 4052 1563 3
8 10 9 7

Starting to write

3

Write between the lines.

Start here

Write between the lines, following the smooth shapes.

Start here

Write between the lines, following the sharp shapes.

Start here

You deserve a shiny star!

4 Writing patterns

Finish the patterns on this roll of wallpaper.
Start from the top of the roll. Write left to right.

Write some of your own patterns to finish the roll.

What lovely patterns!

Writing the alphabet

Write the letters of the alphabet.
For each letter, start at the dot, and follow the arrow.

a a   b b

c c   d d

e e   f f

g g   h h

i i   j j

k k   l l

m m   n n

o o   p p

Super work!

6 Writing the alphabet

q q   r r

s s   t t

u u   v v

w w   x x

y y   z z

Write the alphabet. Write each letter on the lines below.

a b c d e f g h i

j k l m n o p q r

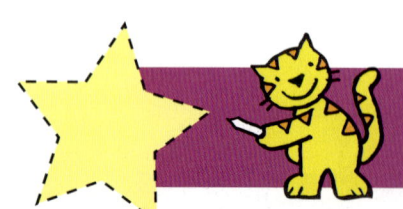

s t u v w x y z

Now you can write all the letters!

Writing letters with 'tails'

7

These letters all have a 'tail'. At the end of each letter the tail turns up to the right, like this:

Write lines of letters. Start at the dots and follow the arrows.

↓• h h

↓• i i   The down stroke of the **i** comes first, the dot last.

↓• k k

↓• l l

↓• m m

↓• n n

↓• t t   The down stroke of the **t** comes first, the little bar last.

↓• u u

Try to make your letters all the same size and shape.

Perfect!

8. Writing letters with 'tails'

The letters m, n and u are the same height. They are shorter than t and k. Write lines of letters.

↓•nk

↓•nt

↓•uk

The 'body' of the letter i is the same height as m, n and u. Its 'head' makes it taller. Write lines of letters.

mi

in

ui

Write lines of words.

lit

hum

kit

nil

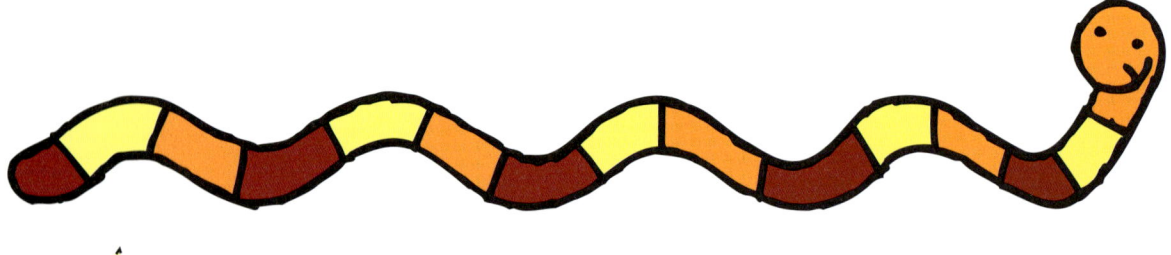

Sssssuper work!

Writing oval letters

These letters are based on an oval shape:

Write the letters. The letters o, c and e are the same height.

o o

c c

e e

Write lines of words.

lock

moon

hole

bee

note

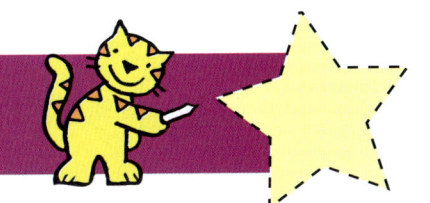

Time for another star!

10 Writing oval letters

The letter a is an oval shape, but with a tail on the right.

The letter d is like a, but with a tall 'handle' on the right.

Write the letters.

a a

d d

Write lines of words.

cat

odd

hide

dad

cola

did

ace

What lovely letters!

Letters with 'handles'

The letters b and p have straight 'handles' joined to an oval.

The letter q has a handle with a tail.

The letter g has a curly handle.

Write the letters.

↓• b b _____

↓• p p _____

↶• q q _____

↶• g g _____

Write the letter sets.

bp _____

pq _____

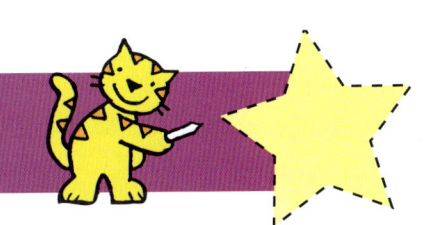

bq _____

gp _____

Note for parents: Make sure tails fall below the line.

12 Letters with 'handles'

Write the letter f in two parts. Write the bar last.

Write the letter j in two parts. Write the dot last.

Write the letters.

ff

jj

Write lines of words.

be

fog

pop

big

jot

quit

jet

Brilliant!

Writing r, s, v, w, x, y and z

The letter r is a straight line with a curl on top.

The letter s is a curly letter.

The letters v, w, x and z are letters based on straight lines.

Write the letters. All the letters are the same height.

r r

s s

v v

w w

x x

z z

The letter y has a curly handle that goes down below the line. Write a line of letter y.

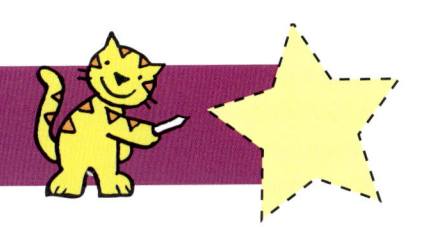

y y

Excellent work!

14 Writing r, s, v, w, x, y and z

Write lines of letter sets.

rs

sw

vwx

xyz

Write lines of words.

stars

yes

x-ray

farm

was

vase

zip

row

Note for parents: Remember to reward your child for effort as well as good work.

Writing capital letters

These capital letters have straight lines.

Write the letters.

↓• I I   ↓• L L

↓• T T   ↓• H H

↓• F F   ↓• E E

These capital letters have curved lines.

Write the letters.

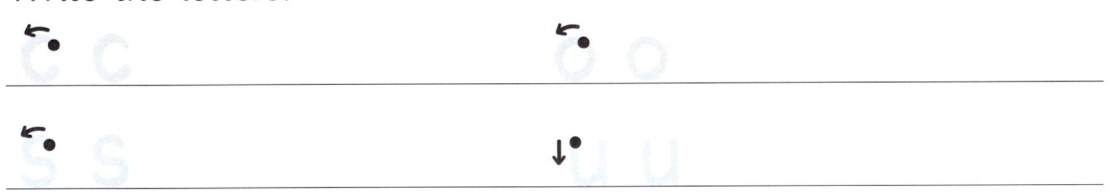

↶• C C   ↶• O O

↶• S S   ↓• U U

Write the letter sets.

S T   O L

C H   E U

F S   C I

You are doing very well.

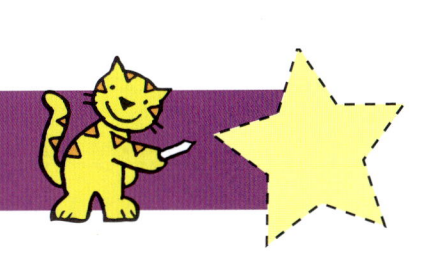

15

Writing capital letters

These capital letters have straight lines and sloping lines.

A K M N V W X Y Z

Write the letters.

A A   K K
M M   N N
V V   W W
X X   Y Y
Z Z

Write lines of capital letters.

TKN
FMV
HYZ
AVN

Note for parents: Practise any letters which your child finds difficult on a separate piece of paper.

Writing capital letters

These capital letters have both straight lines and curved lines.

Write lines of letters.

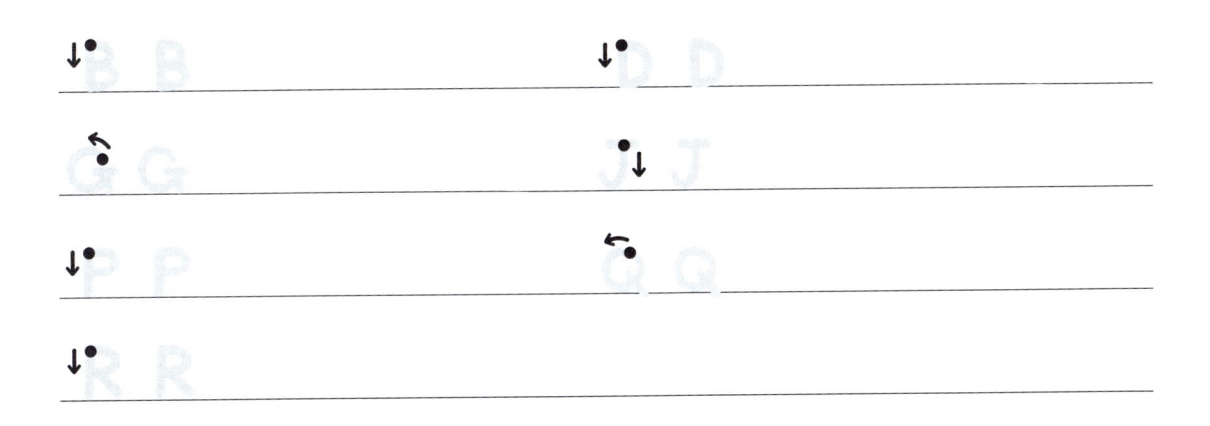

↓• B B   ↓• D D

G G   J↓ J

↓• P P   Q Q

↓• R R

Copy the words on the shopping list.

FISH

CREAM

TINNED MICE

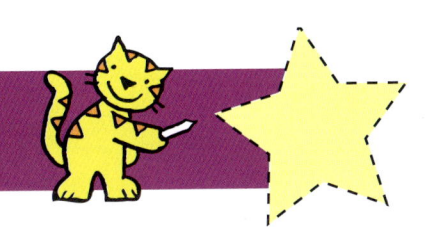

CHOCOLATE

Let's go shopping!

18. Writing capital letters

Write the alphabet in capital letters.

A B C D E F G H I

J K L M N O P Q R

S T U V W X Y Z

Now write in the missing capital letters.

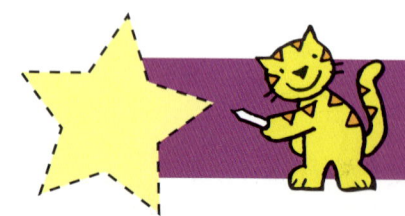

A B C D E _ G H I

J K L _ N _ P _ R

S T _ V W _ Y _

That was easy!

Using capital letters

⭐ 19

Jenny Brown's initials are J. B.

Write the initial letters for these names in capital letters. Remember to put a full stop after each letter.

Tom Smith
Avinder Patel
Lara Marie Jones
William Wilfred Watson
Henry Isaac Sidney Snake

Write your initials here. _____

Abbreviations are written in capital letters. Copy them.

R.S.P.B.   S.O.S.   B.B.C.   ITV

Do you know any others?

Do you know your own initials?

20 Using capital letters

Words on signs that give information are often written in capital letters. Copy these words in capital letters until the end of the lines.

EXIT

DANGER

STATION

SCHOOL

BUS STOP

POST OFFICE

Names of streets and roads can be written in capital letters. Write lines of place names in capital letters.

NEW STREET

LONG LANE

HILL HOUSE

Write the name of your street in capital letters.

Super work!

Joining letters

21

These letters have little tails which make them easy to join.
To join them: write the letter, but don't lift your pencil off the paper. Instead, carry on to the start of the next letter.
Write lines of joined letters.

hu   hu

un   un

nu   nu

The letter k can be written in two different ways.
Write a line of each kind of joined letter k.

kn   kn

kn   kn

Write lines of joined letters.
Dot each i and cross each t when you have finished the join.

it   it

it   it

nt   nt

Note for parents: Make sure your child keeps the pencil on the paper when joining letters.

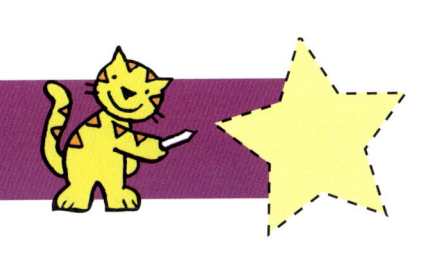

22 Joining letters

Write lines of joined-letter words. Keep your pencil on the paper to the end of each word.

hut

lit

kiln

kilt

mill

milk

tilt

hint

link

thin

think

Super handwriting!

Joining letters

23

These are the oval letters. To join them: write the letter, but don't lift your pencil off the paper. Instead, carry on to the start of the next letter.

Write lines of joined letters.

ce _____

ea _____

ca _____

ed _____

ad _____

The letter o joins from the top. Write lines of joined letters.

od _____

co _____

oc _____

do _____

Keep your pencil on the paper!

24 Joining letters

Write lines of joined-letter words.

dad

mean

made

take

late

the

toe

coat

lot

old

tune

doll

You can write lots of words!

Joining letters

25

These letters join at the top.
Write lines of joined letters.

wi

wr

va

rr

Write lines of joined-letter words.

wave

race

rule

what

have

wild

van

Choose a sticker badge or a star!

26 Joining letters

You can join the letters g, j and y by making their tails into a loop. Write lines of joined letters.

go

yo

je

Now, can you write lines of joined-letter words?

gone

get

joke

yet

you

game

age

Note for parents: Make sure the tails on these letters always fall below the line.

Joining letters

27

You can join the letter q like this.
The letter q is normally followed by the letter u.
Write a line of joined letters q and u.

queen

qu

The letter f joins from the cross bar.
Write lines of joined letter f.

fe

fi

fo

fun

Write lines of joined-letter words.

quilt

fun

fly

face

quiet

Great work! Have a star!

28 Joining letters

The letters b and p can be joined from the base.
Write lines of joined letters.

bbb

ppp

Write lines of joined-letter words.

bed

pen

book

The letters s, x and z can be written in different ways.
Write lines of words with s, x and z.

dress   or   dress

fox   or   fox

exit   or   exit

zip   or   zip

shops   or   shops

Excellent handwriting!

Writing numbers

29

Here's how to write the number words from one to twenty. Can you write them all?

one _____   eleven _____

two _____   twelve _____

three _____   thirteen _____

four _____   fourteen _____

five _____   fifteen _____

six _____   sixteen _____

seven _____   seventeen _____

eight _____   eighteen _____

nine _____   nineteen _____

ten _____   twenty _____

Now you can write numbers!

30 Writing days and months

Write the names of the days in joined-up letters.

Write the names of the months in joined-up letters.

M _____
T _____
W _____
T _____
F _____
S _____
S _____

J _____
F _____
M _____
A _____
M _____
J _____
J _____
A _____
S _____
O _____
N _____
D _____

Excellent! Choose a shiny star!

Writing names and addresses

31

Writing is a mixture of small and capital letters.
Names and places start with a capital letter.
Copy these names and addresses in joined-up writing.

Little Miss Muffet
Curd Cottage
Tuffet Town
Nurseryland
NL1 CC2

T. Rex
Dinosaur Drive
Rockville
Fossil City
FO9 SS3

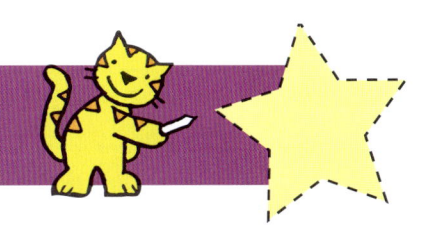

Have you ever sent a postcard?

32 Lettering

At the toy sale you can buy:

In your best handwriting, write out a list of all the things you can buy. Decide the prices yourself and write them on the list.

SCHOOL TOY SALE

Books 10p

The sale starts at 10 o'clock.
Decide where this information should go on your poster, and write it in capital letters.

Note for parents: This tests your child's ability to use capital and lower-case letters appropriately.

excellent   top marks   well done   wonderful work

fantastic   good effort   brain box   clever kid